EARLY
VICTORIAN

CONSTANCE M. GREIFF

ABBEVILLE
STYLEBOOKS™

ABBEVILLE PRESS · PUBLISHERS
NEW YORK · LONDON · PARIS

CONTENTS

Introduction 6

Nobody who has paid any attention to the peculiar features of the present era, will doubt . . . that we are living at a period of transition, which tends rapidly to accomplish that great end, to which, indeed all history points—the realization of the unity of mankind.
—Prince Albert, speech at lord mayor's banquet, 1850

hen the young Victoria ascended to the throne in 1837, both her realm and other industrializing nations had embarked on a remarkable era of peace, progress, and prosperity. The turmoil of the Napoleonic Wars was over; despite revolutionary outbursts in Europe in 1848, the Crimean War in 1853–55, and the American Civil War in 1861–65, a sense of security and confidence pervaded the first thirty-five years of Victoria's reign.

The industrial revolution was well under way. Factories had begun to produce a torrent of useful and luxury goods that brought new standards of comfort to the lives of millions. A glittering bazaar with dozens of choices for every type of commodity was laid out for consumers. Yet at the same time that people expressed a strong belief in the ongoing improvement of society, they also embraced a romantic yearning for what they perceived as the simpler virtues of the past and for the lure of other cultures. Architecture and the decorative arts responded by mining new discoveries about ancient and distant civilizations, as well as the styles of more recent times. The result was a heady brew, with ingredients from ancient Egypt and Rome, medieval England, Renaissance Italy, royal France, and the Near East.

The early Victorian period was an era of tremendous creative energy, particularly in literature and music. This was the golden age of the novel. Readers eagerly awaited the next tale from such authors as Sir Walter Scott, William Makepeace Thackeray, Charles Dickens, Anthony Trollope, Charlotte and Emily Brontë, James Fenimore Cooper, Nathaniel Hawthorne, Herman Melville, Leo Tolstoy, Fyodor Dostoyevsky, and Alexandre Dumas, father and son. Poetry also flourished, with the verse of Robert and Elizabeth Barrett Browning, Alfred, Lord Tennyson, and John Greenleaf Whittier reaching wide audiences, while Walt Whitman remained unappreciated. Music burst out of the narrow confines of aristocratic chambers and small opera houses. Symphonies and concertos by Ludwig van Beethoven and Franz Schubert led the way early in the century; the repertoire was soon enlarged by Felix Mendelssohn, Robert Schumann, and Franz Liszt. Romantic and heroic operas by Gioacchino Rossini, Giacomo Meyerbeer, Giuseppe Verdi, and Richard Wagner tugged the heartstrings and made spirits soar.

In 1850 Prince Albert, Victoria's consort, promoted the idea of a Great Exhibition as a celebration of Britain's progress and industrial might. Opening in London in 1851, the exhibition was housed in the Crystal Palace, designed by Sir Joseph Paxton. A shimmering structure of thin iron members and great panels of glass, the Crystal Palace was itself a tour de force of the new technology. Its exhibits, concentrating on lavish examples of the decorative arts, undoubtedly whetted the acquisitive appetites of viewers. The Crystal Palace symbolized both the rise of industry and Victorians' belief in the promise that the union of technology and art would produce a better life.

THE AGE OF CHANGE

No period in Western history witnessed more rapid change than the early Victorian era of the 1830s to the 1870s. At its start people and materials moved by foot, horse, or sail, and most products were made at home or in small workshops. By its end, steam propelled travelers and commerce, and mechanized factories poured out endless goods. New building types served changed circumstances and aspirations but looked to the past for inspiration.

Cast and wrought iron formed the fabric of publisher Harper and Company's new plant, shown in *Harper's New Monthly* in 1865 with its mechanized presses.

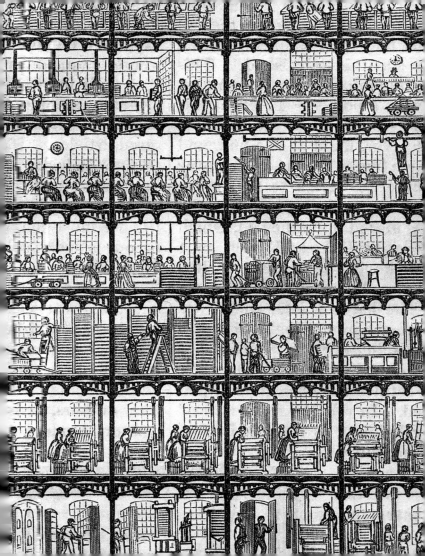

The seeds of the industrial revolution were sown in the eighteenth century, but its fruits were reaped in the nineteenth. Coal fueled steam power for trains, ships, and factories producing every kind of useful and decorative item. Mass production enabled an expanding middle class to buy goods once available only to the wealthy.

Industrial progress profoundly affected the surroundings in which people lived and worked. Streets, public buildings, and some homes were brightened by gaslight. Central heating provided new comfort and led to open plans with free-flowing interior spaces. Improved transportation brought exotic building and decorating materials within reach. Advancements in iron manufacturing allowed engineers to bridge hitherto daunting spans for the new railroads. These advances, combined with new technology for rolling glass in large dimensions and curved sections, made possible huge conservatories, enormous exhibition halls, and great train sheds.

New techniques for manufacturing paper and mechanizing printing created an expanded flow of ideas. Designers and architects could now disseminate theories and plans to thousands, rather than a select few.

Prince Albert (above) was the guiding spirit behind London's Crystal Palace (1851, Sir Joseph Paxton), the prototype for mid-nineteenth-century international exhibitions. Its great transept displayed the soaring possibilities of iron-and-glass construction (opposite).

Later Crystal Palaces
New York City, 1853
Dublin, 1853
Paris, 1855

English explorer Richard Burton, following the route of Arab slave traders in his search for the source of the Nile, sighted Lake Tanganyika on February 13, 1858.

Two generations of explorers—the young Henry Morton Stanley and the older David Livingstone—met in Africa near Lake Tanganyika in 1871.

Even before Victoria became queen, explorers and artists had whetted the public's interest in far-off places. Beginning in the mid-eighteenth century, lavish publications revealed the glory that was Greece and the grandeur that was Rome. Later, artists who had accompanied Napoleon on his Egyptian campaign revealed the secrets of the pharaohs. With the end of the Napoleonic Wars in 1815, wealthy Britons and some Americans could once again embark on the Grand Tour to see for themselves the landscape and architecture of Greece and Italy.

Between 1830 and 1860 Britons planted the flag in exotic climes. They colonized the cape of Africa, New Zealand, Hong Kong, and India. In the 1850s British explorers and missionaries penetrated the heart of Africa, searching for the source of the Nile and discovering Victoria Falls and Lake Tanganyika.

In the United States frontiersmen pushed steadily westward, displacing the native inhabitants. The Louisiana Purchase of 1803 had more than doubled the new nation's size. By 1867, when the country was reunited following the Civil War, it encompassed thirty-seven states; Texas and California were among the thirteen admitted to the Union after 1836.

George Cruikshank

A THIRST FOR REFORM

Victorian prosperity and progress had a dark underside. While the middle class flourished, the poor, including women and children, worked in unhealthy, dangerous mines and factories. Many agricultural workers were held in poverty by rapacious, rent-gouging landlords or, in America, were bound in slavery. Cities grew and slums proliferated, with the accompanying evils of crime and disease. Epidemics had no respect for class; Prince Albert died of cholera in 1861.

While many remained complacent or benefited from these conditions, a multitude of voices championed improvements in living and working conditions for the poor, universal male suffrage, reform of the judicial and penal systems, better care for the ill and insane, education for all, and the abolition of slavery. Gradually, governments took action in response to the reformers; in America the Civil War finally resolved the issue of slavery.

Critics also called for reform in architecture and the decorative arts. A.W.N. Pugin and John Ruskin promoted the Gothic Revival for its beauty and embodiment of the values of a more virtuous past. Less doctrinaire critics were not wedded to a particular style but still defined beauty in moral terms.

Charles Dickens, the most popular storyteller of the period, explored many reform issues in novels such as *Oliver Twist* (1837). The architectural response took the form of model housing, new schools—often Gothic in style like St.-Giles's-in-the-Fields National School (1860, Edward M. Barry) in London—and portentous Egyptian Revival prisons by John Haviland in Trenton, New Jersey (1836), and New York City (1838).

Let us reform our schools, and we shall find little reform needed in our prisons.
—John Ruskin,
Unto This Last, 1862

	1828	1830	1832	1834	1836	1838	1840	1842	1844	1846	1848

POLITICS & SOCIETY

- First railroad into Paris begins service
- Manchester-Liverpool Railroad opens
- *Godey's Lady's Book* published
- English Reform Act passed
- Baltimore & Ohio Railroad opens
- Victoria ascends throne
- *Great Western* uses steam to cross Atlantic
- Daguerreotype perfected
- Plate-glass process refined
- Rubber vulcanization process developed
- Queen Victoria marries Prince Albert
- Morse invents telegraph
- Potato famine devastates Ireland
- *The Condition of the Working Class in England* (Engels)
- Howe's sewing machine patented
- Mexican-American War begins
- *Communist Manifesto* (Marx)
- Revolutions break out in Europe
- California gold rush begins

LITERATURE & PERFORMING ARTS

- *The Hunchback of Notre Dame* (Hugo)
- *Lady of Shalott* (Tennyson)
- Twelve Etudes, Op. 10 (Chopin)
- *Oliver Twist* (Dickens)
- French actress Rachel debuts
- Tom Thumb tours England
- *The Three Musketeers* (Dumas)
- *The Damnation of Faust* (Berlioz)
- *A Book of Nonsense* (Lear)
- *Jane Eyre* (C. Brontë)
- *Wuthering Heights* (E. Brontë)
- *Vanity Fair* (Thackeray)
- Edwin Booth debuts
- Paganini dies
- P. T. Barnum opens American Museum

VISUAL ARTS & DESIGN

- Mount Auburn Cemetery (Bigelow)
- *Encyclopedia of Architecture* (Loudon)
- Halls of Justice (the Tombs) (Haviland)
- Laurel Hill Cemetery (Notman)
- Houses of Parliament begun (C. Barry)
- *Treatise . . . on Landscape Gardening* (Downing)
- *True Principles of Architecture* (Pugin)
- Lyndhurst (Davis)
- *Rain, Steam, and Speed* (Turner)
- Ashmolean Museum, Oxford (Cockerell)
- Trinity Church (Upjohn)
- The Athenaeum, Philadelphia (Notman)
- *The Seven Lamps of Architecture* (Ruskin)
- Osborne House (T. Cubitt)

	1828	1830	1832	1834	1836	1838	1840	1842	1844	1846	1848

1850	1852	1854	1856	1858	1860	1862	1864	1866	1868	1870	1872

POLITICS & SOCIETY

- ■ Napoleon III becomes emperor
- Pullman sleeping car developed ■
- ■ Lincoln assassinated
- ■ First Otis elevator installed
- ■ Civil War ends
- ■ Crimean War begins
- ■ Transatlantic cable laid
- Livingstone discovers Victoria Falls
- ■ Burton discovers Lake Tanganyika
- *Das Kapital* ■ (Marx)
- ■ *The Subjection of Women* (Mill)
- Paris Exposition ■
- ■ India becomes crown colony
- U.S. acquires ■ Alaska
- ■ U.S. transcontinental railroad completed
- *Origin of Species* ■ (Darwin)
- ■ Florence Nightingale founds nursing school
- ■ U.S. Civil War begins
- ■ Suez Canal opened
- Petroleum discovered ■ in Pennsylvania
- ■ Prince Albert dies of cholera

LITERATURE & PERFORMING ARTS

- ■ Tennyson named poet laureate
- ■ *Tristan und Isolde* (Wagner)
- *Sonnets from the Portuguese* ■ (E. Browning)
- ■ *Les Miserables* (Hugo)
- *The Scarlet Letter* ■ (Hawthorne)
- *Crime and Punishment* ■ (Dostoyevsky)
- ■ Jenny Lind makes U.S. debut
- *Blue Danube* (Strauss) ■
- ■ *Moby-Dick* (Melville)
- *Little Women* (Alcott) ■
- ■ *Uncle Tom's Cabin* (Stowe)
- *War and Peace* (Tolstoy) ■
- ■ *La Traviata* (Verdi)
- *The Innocents Abroad* ■ (Twain)
- ■ *Bleak House* (Dickens)
- *Walden* ■ (Thoreau)
- ■ *Leaves of Grass* (Whitman)
- *Middlemarch* (Eliot) ■
- ■ *The Warden* (Trollope)

VISUAL ARTS & DESIGN

- ■ Crystal Palace, London (Paxton)
- ■ Plan for the Paris Opera (Garnier)
- ■ *Death of Ophelia* (Millais)
- ■ Corcoran Gallery (Renwick)
- ■ Plan for Paris (Haussmann)
- ■ Virginia Military Institute (Davis)
- Bibliothèque ■ Nationale Reading Room begun (Labrouste)
- ■ Haughwout Building (Gaynor)
- ■ Leeds Corn Exchange (Brodrick)
- ■ Vassar College (Renwick)
- Balmoral Castle ■ rebuilt
- ■ New Louvre (Visconti and Lefuel)
- ■ Old City Hall, Boston (Gilman and Bryant)
- ■ Vienna Ringstrasse
- Albert Hall ■ (H.Y.D. Scott)
- Smithsonian ■ Institution (Renwick)
- ■ Plan for Central Park (Olmsted and Vaux)
- Albert Memorial ■ (G. G. Scott)
- ■ *Derby Day* (Frith)

1850	1852	1854	1856	1858	1860	1862	1864	1866	1868	1870	1872

A FEAST FOR THE EYES

Victorians had an insatiable appetite for pictures. English aristocrats had long commissioned portraits and purchased old masters; F. X. Winterhalter painted the royal families of England and France many times. But middle-class taste favored paintings telling a contemporary, preferably sentimental story. The Pre-Raphaelites, among them Dante Gabriel Rossetti and Holman Hunt, painted Christian and medieval historical scenes in tones that glowed like stained glass.

The great era of English landscape painting ended with Joseph M. W. Turner's death in 1844. Landscape painting, however, flourished in America, where the Hudson River School painters—Asher B. Durand, Thomas Cole, Henry Inman, and Frederic E. Church—depicted romantic images of a virgin land.

Technology made pictures available to almost everyone. Perfection of chromolithography produced brightly colored copies of paintings, as well as original designs, to adorn cottage walls. Books and popular magazines were crammed with engravings. By the 1840s photography made portraits of loved ones available to the less affluent; later photographs brought home the horrors of the Crimean and Civil Wars with stunning immediacy.

Narrative paintings were particularly popular with early Victorians. John Everett Millais's *Peace Concluded* (1856) depicts a wounded officer returned to home and family.

Popular Paintings

Asher B. Durand's *Kindred Spirits* (1849)

Holman Hunt's *Light of the World* (1853)

George Caleb Bingham's *Verdict of the People* (1855)

William Powell Frith's *Derby Day* (1858)

By May 1852, when *Godey's Lady's Book* showed this morning dress and carriage dress, fullness in the sleeves had migrated downward, from below the shoulder to above the wrist. Rich fabrics included fine woolens, silks, and laces.

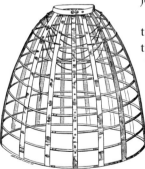

The enormous skirts of midcentury were supported by metal hoops like this one, advertised in *Godey's* in 1858.

Although high-style fashion changed from the 1830s to the 1870s, the principles of beauty in a woman's silhouette remained constant. Narrow, sloping shoulders and pinched waists were a dramatic contrast to long, full skirts. Skirts grew steadily wider. In the late 1860s trains began to appear on street dresses as well as ball gowns. Women drew their hair back and arranged it smoothly over the ears or in side curls. For streetwear, bonnets framed the face. In the evening, ribbons, flowers, and jewels might be added to the coiffure.

Men's clothing acquired modern characteristics. Knee breeches gave way to long trousers, often lighter in color than the coat. The tail coat disappeared, except for evening, replaced by a frock coat; under it was a waistcoat and a shirt with a high collar and a stock or wide bow tie. Hair was generally worn short, but many styles of mustache and sideburns proliferated; beards were less frequent. The top hat was the essential headgear for a man of style.

Shawls, often cashmere, handwoven and embroidered in India, were worn by both men and women. Colorful oriental styles were copied in machine-woven shawls, many made in Paisley, Scotland.

AN ARRAY OF STYLES

Faced with almost incomprehensibly rapid change in their surroundings and society, Victorians turned to the remote in time and space. The growing middle class sought to escape the ills of industrialization and also to validate itself by association with past glories. People chose to live in houses evocative of Italianate villas or Gothic castles, work in Italian palazzos, and worship in medieval-style churches.

The Architect's Dream (1840), painted for the architect Ithiel Town (1784–1844) by Thomas Cole, depicts the architect reclining on a pillar, while choices are spread before him—the classical world to his right, the medieval world to his left.

PAINTED BY ...
FOR ... TO...

In the early nineteenth century, English writers such as Robert Lugar, J. B. Papworth, P. F. Robinson, and Charles Parker began to churn out books illustrating picturesque villas and cottages. Their ideas were popularized by John Claudius Loudon, whose *Encyclopedias* and *Architectural Magazine* were influential in both Britain and America.

Loudon in turn inspired Andrew Jackson Downing, a Newburgh, New York, landscaper who became America's prime apostle of the picturesque. Downing's 1841 *Treatise on . . . Landscape Gardening* introduced Gothic Revival designs by A. J. Davis and an Italianate villa by John Notman. It was wildly successful, going into seven editions published into the 1880s. Downing produced two more books, *Cottage Residences* (1842) and *The Architecture of Country Houses* (1850). A spate of other pattern books appeared between 1849 and 1870 by architects including Samuel Sloan, Calvert Vaux, and Gervase Wheeler.

Magazines also disseminated the cult of the picturesque. London publisher Rudolf Ackermann's *Repository* and Philadelphian Louis Godey's *Lady's Book* offered their readers the latest styles in interior decorating as well as architectural designs.

John Nash (1752–1835) remodeled the Brighton Pavilion (1815–23) for the Prince Regent. Its highly romantic, orientalized design was a precursor of Victorian revivals. Even the kitchen was exotic, with the roof partly supported by elongated palm tree columns.

Form Follows Function

Houses: Tuscan villas and Gothic castles or cottages

Commercial buildings: Italian Renaissance

Churches: Gothic Revival

Colleges: Collegiate Gothic

Prisons and cemeteries: Egyptian Revival

So ubiquitous were brackets on eaves, porches, doors, and windows—as in this house design by John Riddell (*Architectural Designs for Model Country Residences*, 1861)—that "bracketed" became a synonym for the Italianate style.

This builder's drawing of an Italianate bay window appeared in *Woodward's National Architect* (1869).

Romantic seventeenth-century paintings of Italian scenery by such artists as Salvator Rosa and Claude Lorrain inspired Victorian-era Tuscan villas. Irregular in outline, these sprawling houses incorporated multiple intersecting wings and one or more three- or four-story towers. Arcaded loggias shaded both first and second floors, while balconies of all sizes graced second-story openings.

For those with more modest budgets, a popular Italianate house type was a simple cube, two stories high, perhaps with an attic lighted by windows in the frieze. Frequently there was a square or octagonal cupola centered on the roof, plus a lower side or rear wing. The villa and its simpler cousin both had low, hipped roofs with broad, overhanging eaves, often supported by brackets.

The Renaissance palaces of Rome and Florence provided the prototypes for clubhouses, banks, commercial and public buildings, and row houses. Most were stone with rusticated ground floors and windows capped with pediments or bracketed heads. Projecting cornices marked the rooflines. In America cast iron frequently replaced stone on the front of Italianate commercial buildings.

FRONT ELEVATION

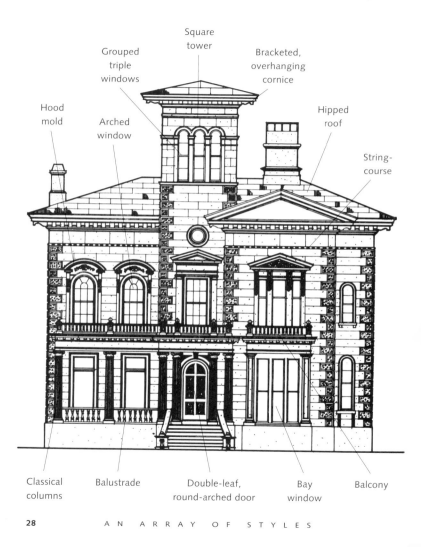

Square tower

Grouped triple windows

Bracketed, overhanging cornice

Hood mold

Arched window

Hipped roof

String-course

Classical columns

Balustrade

Double-leaf, round-arched door

Bay window

Balcony

ITALIANATE FEATURES

Plans and massing:
Variously irregular, with intersecting volumes (villa style); L-shaped; or symmetrical and rectangular, often cubical (bracketed style).

Roofs: Low-pitched, hipped or gabled, sometimes with a central cupola or belvedere; broad overhangs supported by brackets.

Towers: Square, rising one to two stories above the main roof; often triple windows in the upper level.

The Morse-Libby House (1863, Henry Austin), Portland, Maine, illustrates the towered villa style of Italianate architecture.

Materials: Stone; brick, frequently stucco-covered, often scored to simulate stone; flush wooden boards or clapboard; cast iron.

Arches: Round, often with projecting keystones.

Doors: Round-arched or rectangular; often double-leaf, with sunken arched or rectangular panels, transoms, and sidelights.

Windows: Single, grouped in pairs or triplets, or grouped in arcaded rows; double-hung or casement; bay windows; french windows.

Columns: Square piers; round in classical orders (Doric, Tuscan, Ionic, Corinthian, with variants on the latter).

Porches: Arcades; loggias; verandas across the front or wrapping around sides; terraces and balconies with classical balustrades.

Ornament: Scrolled brackets on cornices and supporting door and window heads and sills; dentils; projecting horizontal stringcourses; foliate scrollwork; striped, projecting concave hoods or roofs over doors, windows, balconies, and porches.

The other predominant style of the early Victorian period—the Gothic Revival—enjoyed the imprimatur of virtue as well as fashion. English authorities like A.W.N. Pugin and the Ecclesiological Society recommended the decorated Gothic of the thirteenth and fourteenth centuries as the only proper style. With its pointed arches, mullioned windows, bundled columns, and rich ornament, it was considered particularly suitable for Anglican, Episcopal, and Roman Catholic churches. Because it incorporated the same principles of picturesque irregularity as the Italianate style, it was also used for castlelike villas.

Alternatives to this "pointed style" were many. Tudor or Elizabethan used the three-centered arch of the fifteenth and sixteenth centuries. Towers were lower, and roofs sported parapets. Siege-strength battlements and square, octagonal, and rounded towers marked castellated or baronial Gothic.

Most common in America was what A. J. Downing called rural Gothic, cousin to the English cottage orné. Roughly symmetrical, these charming houses featured steeply pointed central cross-gables, elaborate bargeboards, entrance porches, clustered chimneys, and board-and-batten siding.

At Roseland (1846, Joseph Collins Wells), Woodstock, Connecticut, a modest rural Gothic cottage facade facing the road masks an ample, sprawling villa behind.

Cottage has a charmingly sweet sound, and is, perhaps, more suggestive of comfortable thoughts than any other word in our language, but that of home.
—William H. Ranlett, *The Architect*, 2, 1851

GOTHIC REVIVAL FEATURES

Plans and massing:
Irregular, with intersecting volumes, or symmetrical; often with a projecting central pavilion.

Roofs: Steeply pitched, gabled, sometimes stepped; occasional intersecting cross-gables or castellated parapets; grouped chimneys.

Towers: Tall, square, octagonal, or round; sometimes with small turrets; topped by finials, pinnacles, or spires.

Materials: Stone; brick with stone trim; clapboard or board-and-batten; less frequently cast iron.

Arches: Pointed (sometimes a simple triangle); Tudor; ogee.

Doors: Pointed or Tudor-arched doorways; doors often double-leaf, with sunken arched panels; sidelights may be diamond-paned.

Windows: Single or grouped; double-hung or casement; arched or flat topped with hood moldings; lancets and wheels; bays and oriels; french windows; tracery; conventional or diamond panes; tinted or stained glass, especially in churches.

Columns: Round, polygonal, or occasionally twisted; sometimes bundled or clustered as multiple shafts; capitals with floral or leaf motifs; in churches and other large buildings, often carrying ribbed vaults.

Porches: Verandas across the front or wrapped around sides, sometimes two-story; occasional Gothic columns and arches or jigsawn scrollwork.

Ornament: Trefoils, quatrefoils, and other cusped shapes; complex moldings; pinnacles and finials with crockets; carvings of leaves, flowers, animal and human forms, grotesques and gargoyles; strapwork; linenfold paneling.

St. Luke's Episcopal Church (1839), Hope, New Jersey, is an early, simple version of the Gothic Revival but nevertheless includes the major features of the style.

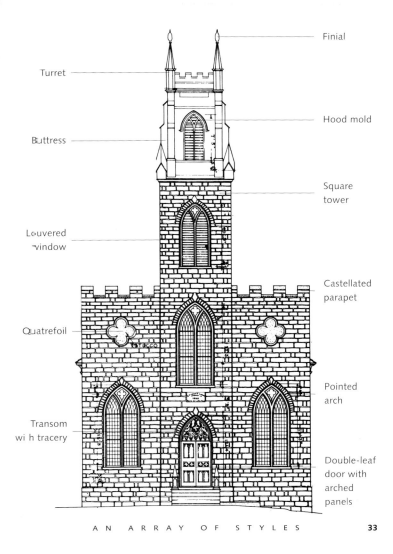

Finial

Turret

Hood mold

Buttress

Square tower

Louvered window

Castellated parapet

Quatrefoil

Pointed arch

Transom with tracery

Double-leaf door with arched panels

Haller Nutt commissioned the Moorish Longwood (1862, Samuel Sloan), Natchez, Mississippi, after seeing a similar design in Sloan's *Model Architect,* 2 (1853).

Alternatives for Victorians who preferred something more exotic than the Italianate and Gothic Revival styles included Romanesque, Egyptian Revival, Moorish, and Swiss cottage.

One Romanesque form, Anglo-Norman, combined the massing and steep gabled roofs of the Gothic Revival with round-arched openings. A similar round-arched style was known as Lombard. Both were considered especially suitable for churches of nonconforming Protestant denominations.

Because of its associations with death, Egyptian Revival was rarely used for houses except for selected furniture pieces. It was, however, thought appropriate for cemetery gates and prisons. Some factories and bridges also sported lotus columns and battered piers of Egyptian ancestry.

Moorish generally was considered cheerful, perhaps because a playful version decked out the Brighton Pavilion (1815–23, John Nash). Its typical use was for houses and some commercial buildings. The Swiss cottage, a distinctly domestic style, was obviously most suitable for a hilly site.

Toward midcentury, elements from various styles were at times combined in eclectic mixes that defy stylistic characterization.

Moorish Style Features

Horseshoe and pointed arches, sometimes multicusped

Slender columns, often grouped

Turrets and minarets

Bulbous or onion domes

Rich surface ornament in geometric, floral, and calligraphic forms

EXOTIC STYLE FEATURES

Swiss Cottage: Gabled roofs with shallow pitches, long slopes, and deep overhangs, sometimes with jerkinhead (clipped) ends; second-story porches and balconies with flat, patterned balustrades; may be sided with shingles or boards applied in rectangular patterns suggesting half-timbering; some stickwork detailing.

Egyptian Revival: Battered (inward sloping) walls and windows; cavetto (concave) cornices; pylon towers; columns with bundled shafts and lotus bud capitals; projecting, rounded torus and roll moldings; vulture and sun disk symbols; pseudo-hieroglyphics; obelisks for memorials.

Romanesque: Round-arched windows, often grouped; round accent windows; gabled roofs; square towers with pyramidal roofs or spires; arched corbels as cornices; friezes and moldings with zigzag or diamond motifs.

Balconies were prominent in William H. Ranlett's design (1849) for a Swiss-style villa (below).

So gloomy was New York City's Egyptian Revival Halls of Justice and House of Detention (1838, John Haviland) (opposite, top) that it was nicknamed the Tombs.

Bartram Hall (1851, Samuel Sloan) (opposite, below), built for a wealthy Philadelphia industrialist, helped popularize the Romanesque or Anglo-Norman style.

Brackets with pendants   Broad overhang

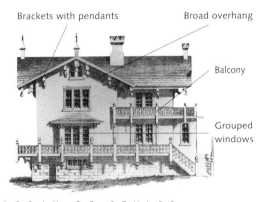

Balcony

Grouped windows

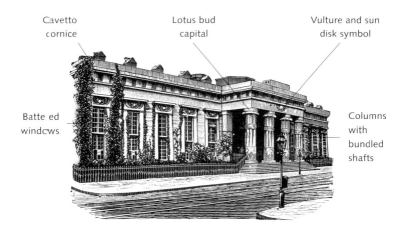

Cavetto cornice

Lotus bud capital

Vulture and sun disk symbol

Batted windows

Columns with bundled shafts

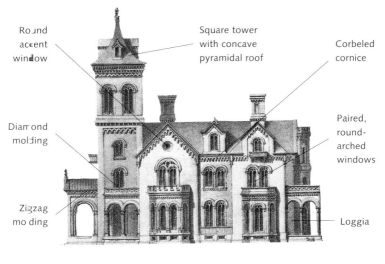

Round accent window

Square tower with concave pyramidal roof

Corbeled cornice

Diamond molding

Paired, round-arched windows

Zigzag molding

Loggia

SECOND EMPIRE

An elaborate mansard tower roof shown in *Woodward's National Architect* in 1869 sported patterned slate and iron cresting.

City Hall Post Office (1875, Alfred B. Mullett), New York City, epitomized the monumental buildings of the post–Civil War period.

In France, Napoleon III came to the throne in 1852. He and his surpassingly beautiful wife, Empress Eugénie, set the fashion in dress as well as architecture. Under him Paris was transformed into a city of broad boulevards lined with imposing buildings. One important project was the New Louvre (1857, Visconti and Lefuel). Evocative although not imitative of the Baroque opulence of Louis XIV's reign, the New Louvre, with its projecting pavilions and deeply undercut attached columns, reintroduced a sculptural quality to architecture.

The most prominent feature of the Second Empire style is a double-pitched mansard roof, usually punctuated by numerous dormers. It was named for a roof type developed by the French architect François Mansart in the seventeenth century. Homeowners especially appreciated it because it provided a full top story at relatively little extra expense.

In the United States the Second Empire became virtually the official style in the 1870s and 1880s. Alfred B. Mullett, the treasury department's supervising architect, used it for government buildings in Washington, D.C., and courthouses, customhouses, and post offices from Maine to Oregon.

SECOND EMPIRE FEATURES

Plans and massing:
Usually symmetrical but
with projecting pavilions
at the center and corners;
sometimes L-shaped.

Roofs: Mansard,
with a lower slope that
is straight, convex,
concave, or S-curved.

Towers: On projecting
pavilions, usually one
story above the building's
main roof.

Materials: Stone;
brick with stone trim
or stuccoed; wood.

Windows: SIngle or
paired; may have large
panes of plate glass;
topped with hood moid-
ings or pediments;
dormers prominent, often
with scrolled hoods and
brackets.

Doors: Segmentally or
round-arched doorways;
often double-leaf.

Columns: Classical,
usually Corinthian or
composite.

Porches: Verandas less
often across the front but
present on sides and rear.

Ornament: Cornices with
brackets and paneled
frieze, crestings, and
finials; carved or incised
decoration; abstract
flower and foliage
designs; S and C curves;
classical motifs.

A late example of the
Second Empire style,
Iolani Palace (1881, T. J.
Baker, C. J. Wall, and
Isaac Moore), Honolulu,
Hawaii, pulled out all
the stops.

Dormer
window

Round-arched
window

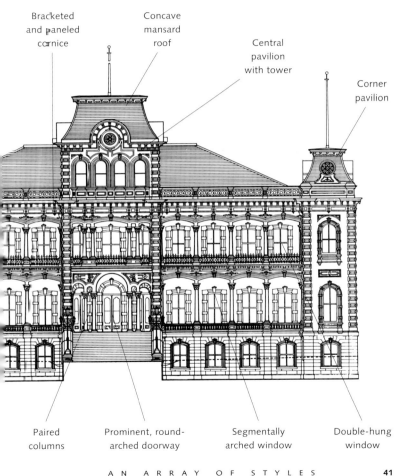

Bracketed
and paneled
cornice

Concave
mansard
roof

Central
pavilion
with tower

Corner
pavilion

Double-hung
window

Segmentally
arched window

Prominent, round-
arched doorway

Paired
columns

ARCHITECTS

Henry Austin (1804–91)
Morse-Libby House (1863),
Portland, Maine

Sir Charles Barry (1795–1860)
Houses of Parliament
(1840–70), London;
Cliveden (1851), near
Maidenhead

Edward M. Barry (1830–80)
Royal Opera House (1857),
Covent Garden, London

**Cuthbert Brodrick
(1822–1905)**
Corn Exchange (1863), Leeds;
Grand Hotel (1867),
Scarborough, Yorkshire

William Burn (1789–1870)
Harlaxton Hall (1838–55),
Lincolnshire;
Falkland House (1844), Fife,
Scotland

Decimus Burton (1800–81)
Palm Stove (1848), Kew

**William Butterfield
(1814–1900)**
Balliol College Chapel (1857),
Oxford

Lewis Cubitt (1799–1883)
King's Cross Station (1852),
London

Thomas Cubitt (1788–1855)
Osborne House (1849),
Isle of Wight

James Dakin (1806–52)
Old Louisiana State Capitol
(1852), Baton Rouge

A. J. Davis (1803–92)
Lyndhurst (1842, 1865),
Tarrytown, N.Y.;
Loudon (1852), Lexington, Ky.

Charles Garnier (1825–98)
Paris Opera (1860–75)

John Haviland (1729–1852)
New Jersey State Penitentiary
(1836), Trenton, N.J.;
Eastern State Penitentiary
(1837), Philadelphia;
Halls of Justice (the Tombs)
(1838), New York

Henri Labrouste (1801–75)
Reading Room, Bibliothèque
Sainte-Généviève (1850), Paris;
Reading Room, Bibliothèque
Nationale (1854–68), Paris

Napoleon LeBrun (1821–1901)
Academy of Music (1856, with
Gustave Runge), Philadelphia

Giuseppe Mengoni (1829–77)
Galleria Vittorio Emanuele II
(1867), Milan

Alfred B. Mullett (1834–90)
Old Executive Office Building
(1871–89), Washington, D.C.

John Notman (1810–65)
The Athenaeum (1847),
Philadelphia;
Hollywood Cemetery (1860),
Richmond, Va.

Sir Joseph Paxton (1803–65)
Crystal Palace (1851), London

**Augustus Welby Northmore
Pugin (1812–52)**
St. Oswald's (1842), Liverpool;
The Grange (1843), Ramsgate

James Renwick (1818–95)
Grace Church (1846),
New York;
Smithsonian Institution (1855),
Washington, D.C.;
Vassar College (1865),
Poughkeepsie, N.Y.

Anthony Salvin (1799–1881)
Peckforton Castle (1850),
Cheshire

**Sir George Gilbert Scott
(1811–78)**
Albert Memorial (1872),
London;
St. Pancras Station and Hotel
(1874), London

Samuel Sloan (1815–84)
Woodland Terrace (1861),
West Philadelphia;
Longwood (1862),
Natchez, Miss.

**William Strickland
(1788–1854)**
First Presbyterian Church
(1851), Nashville, Tenn.

Richard Upjohn (1802–78)
Trinity Church (1846),
New York;
St. Paul's Church (1856),
Baltimore

Thomas U. Walter (1804–87)
Society Hill Synagogue (1830,
1851), Philadelphia;
U.S. Capitol Dome (1865),
Washington, D.C.

Frank Wills (1822–56)
St. Anne's Chapel (1847),
Fredericton, New Brunswick,
Canada

WRITERS & CRITICS

A. J. Davis (1803–92)
Rural Residences (1837)

**Andrew Jackson Downing
(1815–52)**
Cottage Residences (1842);
*The Architecture of Country
Houses* (1850);
Rural Essays (1853)

**Louis Antoine Godey
(1804–78)**
Godey's Lady's Book
(1830–98)

Owen Jones (1806–89)
Grammar of Ornament (1856)

**John Claudius Loudon
(1733–1843)**
An Encyclopedia of Gardening
(1822);
*An Encyclopedia of Cottage,
Farm and Villa Architecture
and Furniture* (1833)

**Augustus Welby Northmore
Pugin (1812–52)**
Contrasts (1836);
*The True Principles of Pointed
or Christian Architecture*
(1841)

William H. Ranlett (1806–65)
The Architect, 1 (1849);
The Architect, 2 (1851)

John Ruskin (1819–1900)
*The Seven Lamps of
Architecture* (1849–51);
The Stones of Venice
(1851–53)

Gottfried Semper (1803–79)
*Die Vier Elemente der
Baukunst* (1851);
Der Stil ... (1863)

Samuel Sloan (1815–84)
The Model Architect, 1 (1852);
The Model Architect, 2 (1853);
*Sloan's Homestead
Architecture* (1861)

Calvert Vaux (1824–95)
Villas and Cottages
(1st ed., 1857; 2d ed., 1864)

**Eugène Viollet-le-Duc
(1814–79)**
Dictionnaire raisonné
(1854–68);
Discourses on Architecture
(1858–72)

Gervase Wheeler (c. 1815–70)
Rural Homes (1851)

LANDSCAPE DESIGNERS

**Andrew Jackson Downing
(1815–52)**
*A Treatise on ... Landscape
Gardening* (1841)

**Georges-Eugène Haussmann
(1809–91)**
Plan for Paris (1853–70)

**Frederick Law Olmsted
(1822–1903) and
Calvert Vaux (1824–95)**
Central Park (1858–78),
New York;
Prospect Park (1865–73),
Brooklyn, N.Y.;
Riverside, Ill. (1870)

Sir Joseph Paxton (1803–65)
Birkenhead Park (1847),
near Liverpool

ENGINEERS

I. K. Brunel (1806–59)
Paddington Station (1854,
with Sir M. D. Wyatt), London

Charles Ellet, Jr. (1810–62)
Niagara Suspension Bridge
(1848), Niagara Falls, N.Y.;
Wheeling Suspension Bridge
(1849), Wheeling, W. Va.

John A. Roebling (1806–69)
Niagara Suspension Bridge
replacement (1855),
Niagara Falls, N.Y.;
Cincinnati Suspension Bridge
(1867), Cincinnati, Ohio;
Brooklyn Bridge (1883),
Brooklyn, N.Y.

Marc Séguin (1786–1875)
Rhône Suspension Bridge
(1824), Tournon

Robert Stephenson (1803–59)
Britannia Bridge (1850),
Menai Straits, Wales;
Victoria Bridge (1859),
Montreal, Canada

PUBLIC LEADERS

**Napoleon III (1808–73) and
Empress Eugénie (1826–1920)**
Rebuilding of Paris (1853–70)

**Queen Victoria (1819–1901)
and Prince Albert (1819–61)**
Osborne House (1849),
Isle of Wight;
Great (Crystal Palace)
Exhibition (1851), London;
Balmoral Castle (1855),
Scotland

Whatever the style of its outer skin, the ideal early Victorian building was picturesque and irregular in plan and silhouette. Towers and turrets were common, and roofs frequently featured a multiplicity of intersecting gables and hips. Where siting or economy made irregularity impossible, symmetry could be rendered picturesque by applied ornament derived from historic styles or disguised by bays, balconies, porticos, and verandas.

Abner Pratt, former consul in the Hawaiian Islands, combined Italianate elements with Hawaiian motifs in Honolulu House (c. 1860), Marshall, Michigan.

Commercial building facades of cast iron made their appearance at midcentury. Although critics recommended otherwise, most cast-iron fronts, like that of New York's City's Haughwout Building (1857, J. P. Gaynor), were painted to resemble stone, a more costly material.

When we employ stone as a building material, let it be clearly expressed; when we employ wood, there should be no less frankness in avowing the material.
—Andrew Jackson Downing, *The Architecture of Country Houses*, 1850

When clients could afford them, stone and brick were preferred materials. The type of stone often depended on the locality. Marble was a luxury; limestone and various forms of sandstone were more common. By the 1840s sober brownstone became popular. Brick frequently was painted or covered with stucco, known as roughcast or mastic. Often this was scored to imitate stone and the lines painted white or gray to imitate mortar.

In the United States wood still dominated. Clapboard continued in extensive use, but board-and-batten emphasized the picturesque verticality and effects of light and shade that expressed the spirit of the age. Planks were laid vertically, their joints covered by narrow plain or beveled strips. On wooden trim, painters sometimes mixed sand with paint to simulate stone.

Paint schemes generally were simple, unlike their later Victorian counterparts. Advice books recommended a range of creams, beiges, and grays. Downing described appropriate colors as "neutral tints being those drawn from nature." Trim was to repeat the base color in a lighter or darker shade. Nevertheless, the critics' repeated condemnation of white suggests that many ignored their advice.

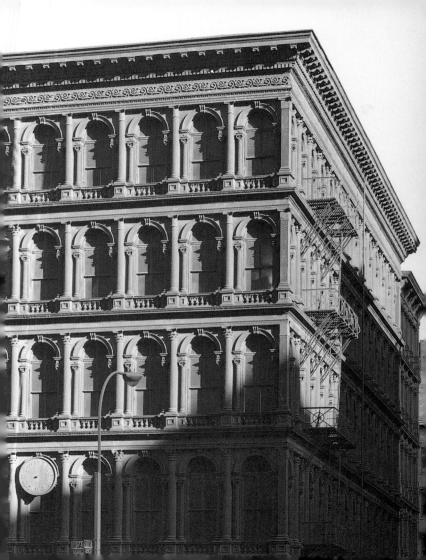

DOORS AND WINDOWS

Victorians accepted nature as a force to be embraced rather than held at bay. They considered doors and windows—where indoors and outdoors met—as vital components of buildings, giving them expression just as eyes, nose, and mouth give expression to the human face.

The main entrance to an early Victorian building was a weighty feature, often set within a deeply recessed porch or portico. Doors were heavy and frequently double-leaf, with arched or rectangular panels framed by substantial moldings. Their sober effect might be lightened by transoms and sidelights with etched or colored glass.

Windows appeared in a dazzling variety, hung singly or in pairs or triplets. Casements returned to fashion, although double-hung sash were still common. Windows might be rectangular or arched, their importance often emphasized by heavy hood molds, small balconies, or gaily striped, flaring metal roofs. Bay windows or upper-story oriels provided variety in silhouette. Floor-length windows with triple-hung sash or french windows with casements opened to the outdoors or to verandas. Inside, shutters, venetian blinds, or shades diffused the light.

The fanciful windows and doorway behind the richly ornamental Moorish portico made a strong design statement at the Willis Bristol House (1845, Henry Austin), New Haven, Connecticut.

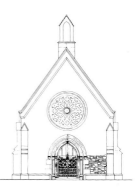

A Gothic rose window dominates the facade of James Renwick's bijou chapel (1850) at Oak Hill Cemetery in Georgetown, Washington, D.C.

PORCHES AND PERGOLAS

The porch, the veranda, or the piazza, are highly characteristic features, and no dwelling-house can be considered complete without one or more of them.
—Andrew Jackson Downing, *Cottage Residences*, 1842

Nothing was more characteristic of early Victorian domestic architecture than an open piazza or veranda. The very words—one Italian, the other East Indian—evoked images of mystery and romance. In variable climates, such as that of North America, a veranda also was practical. It protected the building from the harshness of the elements—wintry blasts and summer heat. In more temperate zones, the unroofed terrace might take its place.

Verandas or terraces were outdoor living rooms, suitable for strolling or sitting. Often they were the most decorative feature of a building. Posts could be either columns appropriate to the building's style or more ornate confections—delicate traceries of cast iron or intricately sawn wood. The spaces between them could be arched or marked by brackets of similar materials.

Ideally the Victorian house was set in a picturesque landscaped garden. The veranda was the intermediary between the building and this landscape, between private and somewhat public space. For those who could afford it, nature could be experienced in a pergola (a rustic or exotic summer house) or coaxed indoors in the form of a conservatory.

OUTSIDE

GARDENS

The English style of landscape gardening was introduced in the eighteenth century by William Kent and Capability Brown and popularized by the poet Alexander Pope. Humphrey Repton carried their principles forward in the early nineteenth century. Applied at first to the parks of great country houses, these theories were brought to wider audiences by Loudon and Downing.

While celebrating nature, the English landscape style also controlled it by artfully contrived means. Trees were removed to enhance vistas, and earth was shaped to create undulating contours. Trees and shrubs were planted in informal clumps scattered about expanses of lawn. Among the most cherished were exotics, such as Cedars of Lebanon or California redwoods. Weeping species also were favored because of the graceful curve of their branches. Winding drives and paths wended through the garden, sometimes leading to a shady retreat—perhaps a seat made of logs or cast iron.

No shrubs or flowers were planted close to building foundations, although vines might climb veranda posts. Flower beds were favored near the house and were often symmetrical, in intricate, geometric patterns.

The front of Prospect (1852, John Notman), Princeton, New Jersey, featured a sweeping lawn with specimen trees. At the rear, terraces spilled down to a semicircular flower garden, complete with radiating paths and geometric beds.

Normally a highly functional object, this ornamental beehive—suitable for the garden—was displayed at London's Crystal Palace.

INSIDE

While the exteriors of early Victorian buildings generally conformed to a single style, interiors were often eclectic. Plans became more open, with spaces flowing into one another. Central heating made possible open plans and high ceilings, at least for the middle and upper classes, and mass production meant that interiors could be crammed with furnishings and objects, producing the comfortable coziness of which Victorians were so fond.

The ideal parlor, depicted in Samuel Sloan's *Model Architect*, 1 (1852), displayed richly decorated and patterned surfaces, as well as a view to the outdoors.

FLOORS, WALLS, AND CEILINGS

Unusually lavish decoration in the Morse-Libby House (1863, Henry Austin), Portland, Maine, included frescoed walls and intricately molded cornices and ceiling panels. The furnishings came from Gustave Herter, founder of Herter Brothers.

Flooring Alternatives

Accent colors—blue, red, and gold in encaustic tile

Dark and light wood laid in alternating stripes or forming patterns

Room-size rugs

Floors were important in interior decorative schemes. The hall floor was sometimes laid in stone or marble squares in contrasting colors. A new substitute for stone was encaustic tile, appearing most frequently unglazed in terra cotta, buff, or black. Tiles were made in squares or octagons, the latter used in conjunction with small squares of contrasting color. A less expensive treatment was a floorcloth (an ancestor of linoleum), painted or printed to simulate stone or carpet. Most other floors were laid with relatively inexpensive, narrow boards, meant to be covered with wall-to-wall carpeting.

A popular treatment for walls was to divide them into panels, not of wood but of paper, paint, or fabric. These generally extended from baseboard to cornice, although at midcentury the dado or wainscot began to reappear. Sometimes the cornice crowning the wall was a paper simulation.

Ceilings could also be laid out in panels of paper or paint, although plaster ribs and coffers alternatively marked ceiling divisions. A ceiling with any pretensions boasted a plaster center flower or medallion, from which a chandelier could hang, as well as plaster moldings around the perimeter.

PAINT AND WALLPAPER

Early Victorian interior paint colors were relatively subdued, although critics recommended a wider range than for the exterior. Hallways, meant to be cool and neutral, were often papered or painted to simulate stone. Parlors and drawing rooms were to be light and gay, dining rooms warm, and libraries subdued. Recommended colors included grays, a variety of "stone" colors, pinks, and pale blues and greens. After midcentury the palette grew deeper; choices such as violet, salmon, and bronze green might be enlivened by touches of gold or silver. Although advice books repeatedly called for honesty in materials, painted graining on pine doors and other woodwork imitated hardwood, while marbleizing enriched baseboards, columns, and entire walls.

Machine-made wallpapers appeared in dazzling variety. Marbleized designs were used to create the popular paneled effect. Architectural papers featured Gothic arches or Italian villas and simulated elements such as columns or realistically shaded cornices.

For those who could afford them, scenic papers remained available. "Le Jardin Japonais" (1861, Victor Poterlet) featured a house that looked suspiciously like an Italianate villa tricked out with pagoda roofs.

The most popular wallpaper patterns were Baroque or Rococo in inspiration. They were embellished with sinuously twining flowers and foliage or undulating S and C curves, like this border from Lindenwald (c. 1850), near Kinderhook, New York.

DECORATIVE TRIM

Wood paneling was used less extensively than in the past, but trim became substantial and heavy. Staircases were prominent, often set in separate stair halls and sometimes screened from the entrance hall by an arcade or columns. Impressive newel posts sat firmly on pedestals; their octagonal or turned shafts terminated in heavy caps. Wood balusters were also turned on machine lathes; occasionally cast iron was used.

Baseboards were high, molded at the top, while door and window frames were broad. In elaborate schemes openings might be topped with round or pointed arches, depending on the building's style. Pattern books favored the use of local hardwoods but found less expensive wood, grained and varnished, an acceptable substitute.

Mantelpieces, some with mirrors reaching to the ceiling, were the focus of most major rooms. Marble was fashionable, but slate, wood, and cast iron were also used and, following the penchant for faux finishes, were frequently painted to look like marble. Simple mantels were framed by plain pilasters, more elaborate models by classical or Gothic columns. Popular round-arched openings bore a cartouche and curving shelves.

Particularly in public buildings, cast iron sometimes took the place of wood or stone trim. These lacy balconies, bookcases, stairs, and lighting fixtures, made by Wood and Perot of Philadelphia, were installed in the Tennessee State Capitol (1859, William Strickland).

A mantel-glass, . . . reaching nearly to the height of the ceiling, always has a more architectural effect than in any other place.
—Andrew Jackson Downing, *The Architecture of Country Houses,* 1850

As indicated by this 1844 advertisement from New York City, plumbing supply houses hastened to fill the demand for bathroom fixtures, as well as pumps, boilers to produce hot water, and improved cookstoves.

For those who could not afford central heating, Downing recommended improved stoves like this coal-burning model.

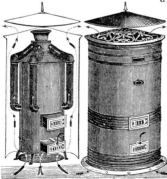

"Modern" conveniences came into general use early in the Victorian period. Central heating and indoor plumbing revolutionized the design and use of buildings. Central heating was first introduced in English mills, factories, hospitals, and asylums in the late eighteenth and early nineteenth centuries. Public buildings followed; in the 1840s central heating was installed in the House of Commons and the White House. By midcentury houses, especially in America, also had this new luxury.

Fireplaces remained popular because of their genial warmth. Closed stoves also were in general use. But neither could supply the pervasive warmth provided by central heating. Hot-air systems were the most common, with a basement furnace producing heat that rose naturally through ducts; floor and wall registers could sometimes be controlled with dampers. Steam and hot-water systems fed into radiators.

Pumps and water-driven rams lifted water to cisterns, from which it flowed to kitchens, laundries, and bathrooms equipped with sinks, flush toilets, tubs, and even showerheads. Still, even large houses rarely had more than one or two bathrooms.

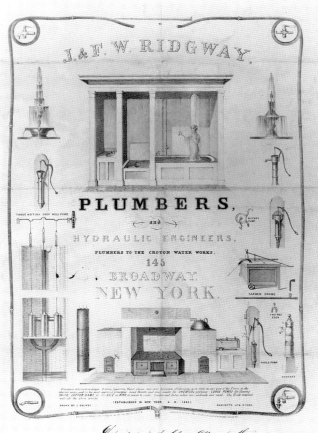

FINISHING TOUCHES

Thanks to mass production, women had a glittering profusion of choices for home furnishings, one sphere in which they generally had free rein and a chance to express personal taste and status. They eagerly intermingled a variety of styles, keeping up-to-date by adding current novelties as fashions shifted. Despite recommendations for simplicity and unity, the well-to-do Victorian home often reflected a yearning for display, ostentation, and magnificence.

At artist S.B. Waugh's house in Bordentown, New Jersey, music enlivened a fashionable parlor, complete with a statue niche and porcelains on an étagère.

Ready-made furniture was available to fit every taste and style. Neoclassical forms remained acceptable, although they became heavier in proportion. Gothic Revival furniture appeared in two basic modes. One featured pointed arches, trefoils and quatrefoils, and crockets and finials. The other, called Elizabethan, was characterized by spool-like or bulbous turnings. Relatively little furniture was made in the Italianate style. Both the Italianate and the Elizabethan lent themselves to "cottage furniture," simplified forms painted in enamel and sometimes stenciled with flowers or other decorative motifs. By midcentury the overwhelming preference was for French Rococo, with its abundance of light, ornamental scrollwork and foliage.

Rich, dark hardwoods, such as mahogany, walnut, and rosewood, were favored, but their effects could also be achieved by graining. New materials were used. Iron made suitable bedsteads for children's and servants' rooms, as well as sometimes elaborate outdoor furniture. Brass was also fashioned into plain or fanciful bedsteads. Rattan was used both indoors and outdoors. Papier-mâché could be formed into graceful shapes, with painted designs and inlaid mother-of-pearl.

Mass production provided furniture en suite for parlors and bedrooms. New furnishing types ranged from large plate-glass mirrors to étagères for displaying the many decorative objects that Victorians cherished. In *Country Houses,* Downing provided illustrations of many furniture styles and types, including this Elizabethan chair and étagère and a Rococo Revival sofa.

There is, at the present moment, almost a mania in the cities for expensive French furniture and decoration.

—Alexander Jackson Downing, *The Architecture of Country Houses,* 1850

Brocades, satins, and velvets provided richness in formal rooms. This damask curtain (opposite) was shown at the Crystal Palace. By 1850 window treatments were increasingly elaborate (below), with Rococo cornices, scalloped lambrequins, and silk and golden cords and tassels.

Cloth manufacture was the first large-scale mechanized process, and a cornucopia of fabrics spilled forth from English, French, and American textile mills. Expanded trade made imported silks and laces readily obtainable. By midcentury improved dyeing techniques provided a spectrum of colors. Fashions in upholstery also changed. Deep tufting offered padded comfort on sofas and chairs, which now sported fringe.

Power looms produced yards of carpeting in narrow strips that were sewn together to fit wall-to-wall. The least expensive and most common were flat-woven Venetians and ingrains. More luxurious was pile carpeting: Axminster, Wilton, Brussels, and tapestry. Florid Rococo patterns were universally popular—despite critics' pleas. Hearth rugs protected carpets in front of the fireplace. Washable floorcloths and oilcloth were popular for heavily traveled spaces such as vestibules, hallways, and kitchens.

Full drapery for windows consisted of inner curtains—of muslin, perhaps patterned, or net bordered with lace—and outer curtains, often of rich fabrics, held back by pins. Straight or arched valances were made of the same material as the outer curtain.

FINISHING TOUCHES

The introduction of centrally supplied coal gas revolutionized lighting in cities and towns. Small, private plants provided gas for the country houses of the rich. Gas gave off brilliant illumination but had to be piped to the lamp. Thus most gas fixtures were chandeliers and sconces, although a table lamp could be supplied by a thin pipe or rubber tube from the gas source in a wall or ceiling.

Candles and lamps remained major sources of light. The Argand lamp, which brightened by forced air, was developed in the late 1700s, but its fuel reservoir, above the burner, cast a shadow. Many nineteenth-century solutions featured a doughnutlike round or oval reservoir surrounding the burner. Known as astral (starlike), solar (sunlike), and sinumbra (shadowless) lamps, these were often tall and took the place of honor on center tables.

There also were endless developments in lamp fuels. One of the most prized oils came from sperm whales and spawned a flourishing New England industry. Kerosene, perfected in the 1850s, was an even more satisfactory fuel. Petroleum, discovered in Pennsylvania in 1859, promised a seemingly inexhaustible supply of oil for its manufacture, so kerosene soon superseded other sources of light.

At the Crystal Palace in 1851, Philadelphia manufacturer Cornelius and Baker exhibited this gas chandelier, one of a pair more than fifteen feet tall.

Lighting Part by Part

Font: Reservoir, usually metal or glass, to hold fuel

Burner: Metal device to hold the wick or feed fuel

Shade: Shield of glass or other material fastened above the light source

Globe: Shield of glass fastened below the light source

Chimney: Glass tube controlling the direction of smoke

Ceramic pedestals and jardinieres accommodated the potted plants cherished in Victorian households.

This globe from Edinburgh, exhibited at London's Crystal Palace in 1851, reflects Victorians' interest in far-off places. Its wooden pedestal is finely carved.

A plethora of objects poured forth from Victorian factories and artisans. Gilded girandoles with glass prisms shared space on deep mantel shelves with clocks, vases, and figurines of pottery, porcelain, and colored glass. Niches in halls and stairways held busts or classically inspired statues. Smaller statuettes stood on pedestals and tables. The best were carved of white Italian marble, but statuary was also mass produced in plaster of paris or parian, an unglazed porcelain.

Tables, often draped in colorful cloths, held myriads of small objects, as did whatnots or étagères. Boxes made of wood and various metals were often elaborately engraved and inset with semiprecious stones. Arrangements of wax or shellwork fruits and flowers were preserved under glass domes. Sideboards, larger and more heavily carved than before, were laden with silver, plate, and engraved or colored glass jugs and decanters.

Middle- and upper-class women, barred from gainful employment, occupied themselves with needlework, especially Berlin woolwork, a form of needlepoint. Their busy hands turned out pen wipers, bookmarks, lamp mats, and other small objects, as well as fire-screen covers and chair upholstery.

I N   S T Y L E

All sorts of new building types—suburban villas, factories, commercial establishments, railroad stations and bridges, hospitals and insane asylums, model workers' housing, colleges, museums, and libraries—were created to meet the demands of a new age. Except for the iron-and-glass exhibition halls, railroad stations, and occasional libraries, most hid new building technology under a skin of one or the other historic styles favored by Victorians.

James Renwick's winning submission in the design competition for the Smithsonian Institution (1855) in Washington, D.C., became known as the Castle.

Prince Albert played an active role in the design of Osborne House (1849, Thomas Cubitt), the royal retreat on the Isle of Wight. The house combines elements from Italian villas and palazzos in a picturesque composition.

Victorian Villas of Note

Montgomery Place
 (additions and alter-
 ations, 1843–67,
 A. J. Davis), Barrytown,
 New York

King Mansion (1847,
 Richard Upjohn), New-
 port, Rhode Island

Cliveden (1851, Sir
 Charles Barry), near
 Maidenhead, England

Johnston-Felton-Hay
 House (1861, Thomas,
 Thomas, and Son),
 Macon, Georgia

In response to Loudon's and Downing's promotion of "rural architecture," many distinguished early Victorian houses graced bucolic settings. In Britain Gothic Revival castles and Italianate villas by architects like Anthony Salvin, Sir Charles Barry, and William Burn populated the countryside. Queen Victoria and Prince Albert chose one of each: Italianate for Osborne House (1849) and Gothic for Balmoral Castle (1855). In America the banks of the Hudson River were lined with castles like Lyndhurst (1842, 1865, A. J. Davis), while the environs of Princeton, New Jersey, were embellished with Italianate villas by John Notman. The most elaborate Moorish house, left incomplete during the Civil War, was Longwood (1862, Samuel Sloan), outside Natchez, Mississippi.

Horsecars and railroads allowed middle-class people to live in suburbs removed from the grime and noise of the industrial metropolis, and romantic revival styles provided models for their ideal homes. Books by Downing, Gervase Wheeler, and Calvert Vaux featured cottages as well as castles. In *The Architect*, 1 (1849) William H. Ranlett offered small villa and garden designs for a suburban lot as small as 15,000 square feet.

Even in the heart of cities, the very wealthy built freestanding mansions. R. S. Morse's magnificent new house in Portland, Maine (1863, Henry Austin), was a "rural" Italianate villa. In some suburbs within the city—London's St. John's Wood, New Haven's Hillhouse Avenue, and Cleveland's Euclid Avenue—individual villas predominated.

For most middle-class city dwellers, however, the high cost of land made only row houses feasible. Attached houses had become the pattern in London after the Great Fire in 1666. Decorous rows and terraces began to characterize the West End in the late 1700s and early 1800s. Often these schemes were not completed until the Victorian era; they were then finished in a conservative manner, only their greater height and amplitude suggesting their true date. In America, as well, Victorian dress was applied to row houses.

Gothic Revival was rare because its picturesque forms did not lend themselves to constant repetition. The Italianate palazzo and later Second Empire, on the other hand, were ideally suited to long, uniform rows. Their bold moldings and strong projecting cornices or mansard roofs helped pull the several units of a row into a unified composition.

For their row houses, Americans favored dark stone like that used for these examples in New York City—so much so that "brownstone" has become virtually synonymous with "row house." In England, following Georgian and Regency precedents, row houses generally were stuccoed and painted in cream or white.

The rich gray and brown stone of every shade, from our native quarries . . . impart an air of quiet gentility to private buildings, of philosophical gravity to those of a public character.
—Philadelphia *Public Ledger,* August 26, 1847

A few factories boasted specific stylistic trappings, like the Italianate Saltaire Mills in Yorkshire (1853, Lockwood and Mawson) and, shown here, an Egyptian Revival flax mill (1840, Joseph Bonomi) in Leeds.

Surviving Specimens

Albert Dock (1845, Jesse Hartley), Liverpool

Jonas Chickering and Sons Factory (1853), Boston

A. Gardner and Son Warehouse (1855, John Baird), Glasgow

Bank of Columbus (1860), Columbus, Georgia

Soho Cast-Iron District (1860s–1870s), New York City

The Victorian age created the modern systems of manufacturing, banking, and capitalism. Industrial complexes mushroomed along river banks and city edges. Some industrialists built towns, such as Lowell, Massachusetts, with company-owned housing, stores, and even cemeteries. Most factories were strictly functional in design, their brick exteriors pierced by rows of windows.

Banks, ever conservative, clung to the Greek Revival, although Philadelphia's Bank of North America (1848, John Notman) established a trend toward the Italianate palazzo, while the Moorish Old Farmers and Exchange Bank (1854, Francis D. Lee) in Charleston, South Carolina, showed a taste for the exotic.

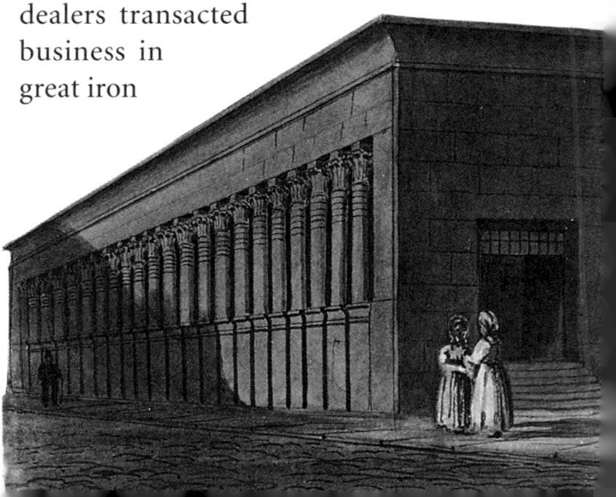

Stock and commodity dealers transacted business in great iron rotundas under soaring glazed domes, like that of the Corn Exchange (1863, Cuthbert Brodrick) in Leeds. Especially in America, cast-iron fronts, occasionally Gothic but usually Italianate, incorporated great expanses of glass, providing natural light to offices and shops. One of the largest, A.T. Stewart's (1862, John Kellum) in New York City, housed an early Victorian invention, the department store.

At Vassar College (1865), Poughkeepsie, New York, James Renwick introduced the Second Empire style as a collegiate alternative to Gothic. Vassar was the first college to offer a full curriculum for women. Its architectural style became a prototype for many land-grant colleges built after the Civil War.

Victorian culture moved from aristocratic collections and exclusive universities into the public domain. Education for all, including middle- and working-class children and women, was an aim that was achieved only gradually with the opening of new schools and colleges. Gothic was the preferred style because of education's associations with the church and the great English universities.

A better-educated populace flocked to new libraries and museums. Karl Marx wrote *Das Kapital* (1867–94), in Sydney Smirke's cast-iron British Museum Reading Room (1857). In Paris readers sat beneath the fan-

tastic Byzantine domes of the Bibliothèque Nationale (1854–68, Henri Labrouste). For the Smithsonian Institution (1855) in Washington, D.C., James Renwick produced an Anglo-Norman castle.

England's memorial to the much-mourned prince consort was a vast cultural complex in South Kensington—irreverently dubbed the "Albertopolis"—begun in 1859. From his perch under the Gothic canopy of the Albert Memorial (1872, Sir George Gilbert Scott), a statue of the departed prince looks down on the Albert Hall (1871, H. Y. D. Scott) and a quadrangle of museums and institutions.

Education must be liberal and comprehensive as well as universal and cheap, or the result will remain incomplete.

— Calvert Vaux,
Villas and Cottages,
2d ed., 1864

In 1858, six years after Downing's tragic death, his partner, Calvert Vaux, and Frederick Law Olmsted won the competition to design New York City's Central Park. H. B. Dodworth's sheet music, published in 1863, shows the park's major attractions: walks and drives, a lake for boating, and a bandstand.

One of the most remarkable illustrations of the popular taste, in this country, is to be found in the rise and progress of our rural cemeteries. . . .
—Andrew Jackson Downing, *Rural Essays*, 1853

The Victorian ideal might have been suburban or rural living, but employment kept large segments of the populace confined to urban areas. Enlightened governments, national and local, sought to provide respite from the noise, dirt, and pollution of the cities. In Paris between 1853 and 1870, Baron Georges-Eugène Haussmann cut bold new avenues through twisting, medieval streets. Lined with handsome shops and apartments, the boulevards provided access to new cultural institutions and to great parks on the outskirts, the Bois de Boulogne and the Bois de Vincennes. Emperor Franz Josef followed suit and in 1858 began to tear down Vienna's ancient walls, replacing them with the Ringstrasse, which included both cultural institutions and great open spaces. In London the royal preserves, including Kew Gardens, Kensington Gardens, and Hyde Park, were thrown open by midcentury.

The American public's first experience of picturesque landscape gardening was at rural cemeteries. They became so popular for drives and strolls that 30,000 people visited Laurel Hill Cemetery outside Philadelphia in 1848. Downing tirelessly advocated English-style parks for American cities.

CENTRAL PARK

MUSIC

LITH. OF THOMAS & ENO. 37 PARK ROW, N.Y.

From minstrel shows to high drama, from circuses to symphonies, Victorians loved a good show. They flocked to see Jenny Lind, Charles Kean, and Rachel, the great French actress. Most artists and repertory companies toured, and by the 1870s most cities had at least one theater or opera house.

Music provided amusement at home —many parlors had a piano—and at large. Romantic symphonies and operas demanded large halls, and government and private enterprise sponsored their construction. Philadelphia's Academy of Music (1856, LeBrun and Runge) and London's Albert Hall (1871, H.Y.D. Scott) were relatively restrained Italianate designs. Nothing approached the Paris Opera (1860–75, Charles Garnier) for opulence. Its imposing entrances, glittering foyers, and anterooms made the spectacle of attendance as much a part of the entertainment as the performance.

Victorians also enjoyed outdoor sports. Riding, rowing, and croquet were suitable even for young ladies. Horse racing drew fashionable throngs to Longchamps, Ascot, and Saratoga Springs, while crowds lined New York Harbor and the Isle of Wight to watch professional crews race sailing yachts.

The English actor Charles Kean enthralled audiences with his portrayal of Hamlet.

Currier and Ives recorded Jenny Lind, the "Swedish Nightingale," making her American debut in 1850 at Castle Garden, a theater built in the shell of an old fort in New York City.

TRANSPORTATION

New building types responded to travelers' needs. The great iron-and-glass train sheds, such as London's St. Pancras (1865, W. H. Barlow and R. M. Ordish), were among the most spectacular constructions of the age.

Short trips were still made on horseback or in horse-drawn carriages like this American one.

Transportation became speedier, if not more comfortable. Between 1830 and 1860, 10,000 miles of rail were laid in England; in 1869 the transcontinental railroad across the United States was completed. Following Robert Fulton's successful steamboat demonstration in 1807, such vessels began to ply America's lakes and rivers. Steam-assisted sailing ships conquered the seas; the first transatlantic crossing entirely under steam was made by the *Great Eastern* in 1858.

Yet travel could be hard and occasionally dangerous. Trains were dirty and noisy, and accommodations on boats primitive. Still, travelers were attracted by convenience and speed. Easier access stimulated the growth of spas like Saratoga Springs and Baden-Baden and seaside resorts like Brighton and Blackpool in England and Cape May, New Jersey, and Newport, Rhode Island.

With so many people on the road, old inns and taverns were no longer adequate. Palatial hotels took their place, some, especially in England, integrated with the stations.

SOURCES OF INFORMATION

**American Institute
of Architects**
1735 New York
Avenue, N.W.
Washington, D.C. 20006

**American Society
of Landscape Architects**
4401 Connecticut
Avenue, N.W.
Washington, D.C. 20008

**L'Association
des Vieilles Maisons
Françaises**
93, rue de l'Université
75005 Paris, France

**The Athenaeum
of Philadelphia**
219 South Sixth Street
Philadelphia, Pa. 19106

**Heritage Canada
Foundation**
P.O. Box 1358, Station B
Ottawa, Ontario
K1P 5R4, Canada

**Historic American
Buildings Survey**
National Park Service
U.S. Department
of the Interior
P.O. Box 37127
Washington, D.C.
20013-7127

**National Monuments
Record**
Fortress House
23 Savile Row
London W1X 2JQ,
England

**National Register
of Historic Places**
National Park Service
U.S. Department
of the Interior
P.O. Box 37127
Washington, D.C.
20013-7127

**National Trust for
Historic Preservation**
1785 Massachusetts
Avenue, N.W.
Washington, D.C. 20036

**National Trust for Places
of Historic Interest or
Natural Beauty**
36 Queen Anne's Gate
London SW1H 9AS,
England

**Society of Architectural
Historians**
1232 Pine Street
Philadelphia, Pa. 19107

Victorian Society
1 Priory Gardens
Bedford Park
London W4 1TT,
England

**Victorian Society
in America**
219 South Sixth Street
Philadelphia, Pa. 19106

ADDITIONAL SITES TO VISIT

See also places cited in the text.

The Athenaeum (1839)
Manchester, England

The Athenaeum (1849)
Boston, Mass.

Bibliothèque Sainte-Geneviève Reading Room (1850)
Paris, France

City Hall (1871–1901)
Philadelphia, Pa.

City Hall (1853)
Utica, N.Y.

Clifton Suspension Bridge (1864)
Bristol, England

Edward King House (1847)
Newport, R.I.

First Presbyterian Church (1851)
Nashville, Tenn.

Gare du Nord (1866)
Paris, France

Grand Hotel (1867)
Scarborough, England

Great Conservatory (1840)
Chatsworth
Derbyshire, England

Harlaxton Hall (1838–55)
Lincolnshire, England

Hotel Belvedere (1857)
Galena, Ill.

Houses of Parliament (1840–70)
London, England

Johnston-Felton-Hay House (1861)
Macon, Ga.

Kingscote (1841, 1881)
Newport, R.I.

The Lace House (c. 1869)
Black Hawk, Colo.

Medical College of Virginia (1844)
Richmond, Va.

Old City Hall (1865)
Boston, Mass.

Old Executive Office Building (1871–89)
Washington, D.C.

Palm House (1848)
Kew Gardens
London, England

Pinakothek (1854)
Dresden, Germany

Soho Cast-Iron District
New York, N.Y.

Travellers' and Reform Club Houses (1832)
London, England

Trinity Church (1846)
New York, N.Y.

Wheeling Suspension Bridge (1849)
Wheeling, W. Va.

RECOMMENDED READING

The Crystal Palace Exhibition. 1851. Reprint. New York: Dover, 1970.

Curl, James Stevens. *Victorian Architecture*. London: David and Charles, 1990.

Dixon, Roger, and Stefan Muthesius. *Victorian Architecture*. London: Thames and Hudson, 1978.

Downing, A[ndrew] J[ackson]. *The Architecture of Country Houses*. 1850. Reprint. New York: Dover, 1969.

Garrett, Wendell D., et al. *The Arts in America*. New York: Scribner's, 1969.

——. *Victorian America.* New York: Rizzoli, 1993.

Gowans, Alan. *Images of American Living*. 1964. Reprint. New York: Harper and Row, 1976.

Hitchcock, Henry-Russell. *Architecture: Nineteenth and Twentieth Centuries*. 1958. 4th ed. Reprint. New York: Penguin, 1977.

——. *Early Victorian Architecture in Britain*. New Haven: Yale University Press, 1954.

Kostof, Spiro. *A History of Architecture*. New York: Oxford University Press, 1985.

Lynes, Russell. *The Art-Makers*. Reprint. New York: Dover, 1982.

Maas, John. *The Gingerbread Age*. New York: Rinehart, 1957.

Moss, Roger W., and Gail Caskey Winkler. *Victorian Exterior Decoration*. New York: Holt, 1987.

Pevsner, Nicholas. *Studies in Art, Architecture, and Design*. Vol. 2. New York: Walker, 1968.

Pierson, William H., Jr. *American Buildings and Their Architects: Technology and the Picturesque*. New York: Doubleday, 1978.

Thornton, Peter. *Authentic Decor*. New York: Viking, 1984.

Winkler, Gail Caskey, and Roger W. Moss. *Victorian Interior Decoration*. New York: Holt, 1986.

INDEX

CREDITS

The Architect, 1 (Ranlett, 1849): 36

The Architecture of Country Houses (Downing, 1850): 62, 66

Journal Illustrated Catalogue (1851): 53, 69, 70, 72, 73, 88

Athenaeum of Philadelphia: 27, 58

Bettmann Archive: 13

Boston Public Library, Fine Arts Department, courtesy Trustees of the Boston Public Library: 8–9; 89 (Building News, 1869)

Godey's Lady's Book: 20 (1858); 21 (1852)

Historic American Buildings Survey: 28, 30, 33, 40–41, 44–45, 47, 48, 49, 51, 60

Leeds City Council: 80–81

Library Company of Philadelphia: 64–65

Library of Congress: 2, 12, 35, 39, 63, 74–75, 87

Minneapolis Institute of the Arts: 18

The Model Architect, 1 (Sloan, 1852): 1, 37 (bottom), 54–55

Museum of the City of New York: 4–5 (Harry T. Peters Collection); 85, 86 (J. Clarence Davies Collection)

National Monuments Record, © RCHME Crown Copyright: 77

The New-York Historical Society: 78

Oliver Twist (Dickens, 1846): 14

Our Police Protectors (Costello, 1885): 37 (top)

Patterson, Flynn and Martin, Inc.: endpapers

Princeton University Libraries, University Archives, Department of Rare Books and Special Collections: 52

The Royal Collection, © Her Majesty Queen Elizabeth II: 11

Royal Pavilion, Art Gallery and Museums, Brighton: 24

Scalamandré: 59

Toledo Museum of Art: 22–23 (Florence Scott Libbey bequest in memory of her father, Maurice A. Scott)

Vassar College Libraries, Special Collections: 82–83

Victoria and Albert Museum Picture Library: 10

Victoria Society of Maine: 57

Woodward's National Architect (Woodward and Thompson, 1869): 26, 38

© Zuber and Cie: 58

Endpapers: Repro-
duction of a floral
carpet from the 1840–
70 period, Patterson,
Flynn and Martin.

Page 1: Summer house
design from Samuel
Sloan's *Model Architect,*
1 (1852).
Page 2: Foyer of the
Paris Opera (1860–75,
Charles Garnier).
Pages 4–5: *American
Country Life: May
Morning* (1855, Currier
and Ives).

Produced by
Archetype Press, Inc.
Project Director:
Diane Maddex
Editor:
Gretchen Smith Mui
Editorial Assistant:
Kristi Flis
Art Director:
Robert L. Wiser

10   9   8   7   6   5   4   3   2   1

Other titles in the Abbeville StyleBooks™
series include *Art Deco* (ISBN 1-55859-824-3);
Arts & Crafts (ISBN 0-7892-0010-4);
and *Gothic Revival* (ISBN 1-55859-823-5).

Library of Congress Cataloging-in-Publication Data
Greiff, Constance M.
Early Victorian / Constance M. Greiff.
    p.   cm. — (Stylebooks)
ISBN 0-7892-0011-2
1. Architecture, Victorian. I. Title. II. Series.
NA645.5.V5G74 1995
724'.5–dc20   94-43148